Pungo Tales Three:

People, Pets, Places

by

Walter A. Whitehurst

An original compilation of tales by the author and others
(Everyone who has told me stories included in this book has given me verbal or written permission to publish them.)

Published by

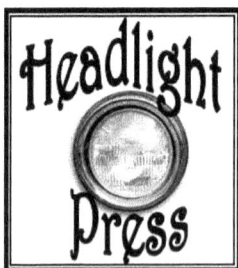

HEADLIGHT PRESS
6500 Clito Road
Statesboro, Georgia 30461

ISBN: 1-58535-261-6

Dedication

It is my pleasure to dedicate this book to the City of Virginia Beach, in honor of its 50th anniversary as a city, resulting from the merger of the town of Virginia Beach and the former Princess Anne County on January 1, 1963. Pungo is a very important part of Virginia Beach, the largest city in Virginia.

TABLE OF CONTENTS

Foreword

Since the publication of *Pungo Tales Two: Some Old, Some New* in March 2012, I have encountered people and circumstances that have generated my interest in putting together new stories for this book, *Pungo Tales Three: People, Pets, Places*. It has been a joy to get better acquainted with the persons interviewed as they have shared their tales. With these new insights, I have grown to appreciate even more all that is involved in living in Pungo.

Portions of Chapter Two, "Growing Up in Pungo," and Chapter Four, "Pungo Pets," are taken from my most recently published book, *Our Life Story: Blessed by God through Mission*, by Walter A. Whitehurst and Betty C. Whitehurst (In His Steps Publishing, Statesboro, Georgia, December 2012).

I want to thank my wife Betty for editing this book, as she has done for my previous books, and to thank our daughter Mónica for proofreading the manuscript this time as she has done in the past. Without their help, this book would not have become a reality. I hope the readers will enjoy these tales.

-- Walt Whitehurst, Pungo,
May 2013

I.

WHY PUNGO
TALES THREE?

STANDING IN HER LIVING ROOM

(As told by Violet Jensen)

I have received many interesting comments from persons who have read copies of my first two books about Pungo. I am sharing some of them in this chapter.

Our friend Violet Jensen said that immediately after she bought my first book, *Pungo Tales*, she took it home and standing in the center of her living room she read much of the book. She just could not put it down.

I hope everyone who reads *Pungo Tales Three* will be equally enthusiastic. Thank you for your interest in learning more about Pungo people, places, and events.

❄

AN EMAIL CONVERSATION

One person who emailed to inquire about ordering my books also asked, "Do you know if Blue Pete's or the Historical Society still has copies of Louisa Venable Kyle's *The Witch of Pungo, and Other Historical Stories of the Early Colonies*? I've written to both and no reply as of today." I wrote back that I was enjoying our correspondence and that *The Witch of Pungo* was usually for sale at the Pungo Strawberry Festival.

She wrote back, "We were at Sandbridge for the week just before the festival and missed it. BUT, we have the article, printed the week before, featuring you [as the Honorary Mayor of Pungo] and your lovely wife [as the Honorary First Lady and Witch of Pungo]. I'm lovin' our correspondence too." When she sent her check for *Pungo Tales* and *Pungo Tales Two: Some Old, Some New*, I wrote back, "The two books have been sent to you in today's mail. I hope you will enjoy reading them."

Her next email said, "Your wonderful stories arrived in today's mail. My husband carried them into the house. Once I opened my envelope, he grabbed them and hasn't put them down since 5:30 p.m. (except to eat supper). He's laughing and crying. Maybe he'll share tomorrow. What a treat. Thank you for writing and publishing these wonderful tales."

THE WRESTLING MATCH

My son Bruce wrote after reading the second Pungo book, "I thoroughly enjoyed reading *Pungo Tales Two*! I know you get a lot of feedback from people you write about, so here is 'the rest of the story' on one story ["Pungo Electronics"] that mentions my brother David and me.

"When Grandpa bought the new TV on the spot, not only were we impressed with the manner in which he did so, but we were also quite impressed that he had the TV bought, delivered and set up in time for us all to watch Mid-Atlantic Championship Wrestling! I believe Grandpa's sense of urgency about buying that TV had a lot to do with the fact that he did not want to miss the wrestling show."

A RESPONSE TO PUNGO TALES TWO

(By Geóbel González, Havana, Cuba)

Our long-time friend Geóbel is a retired lawyer who speaks English as well as Spanish. We sent him copies of both *Pungo Tales* books, and here is what he wrote:

"Reading this second volume was refreshing, leaving me with a sensation very similar to the one that remains with me after a meeting with old friends where we tell stories about our home town and its people. It occurs to me that Walter did the same thing that happened at the wedding in Cana, where they reserved the best wine for the last, reserving the most entertaining stories for the 'Final Word from the Author' at the end of the book. I laughed heartily as I imagined those situations described, and at the same time I remembered the many occasions in which I have seen myself in similar straits.

"One thing both volumes of *Pungo Tales* have in common is the permanent presence of Joe Burroughs, who besides having a prodigious memory and being an excellent recounter of stories, seems to have been the author's companion in mischievous pranks. . . . I will permit myself to make a joke at his expense, although I do not know him personally; he probably should not visit Báguanos [Geóbel's home town in Cuba] because they would most likely Cubanize his surname, pronouncing it phonetically, and the result would be 'burros' ['donkeys']."

HIGH SCHOOL SHOP CLASS AND THE WOODEN PADDLE

(Revisited by Sonny Hollis, Lamesa, Texas)

Some readers of *Pungo Tales Two: Some Old, Some New* may remember the story about "Tommy Tomko and The Shop Class." We sold a copy of the book to my wife Betty's high school friend, Sonny Hollis, and he related immediately to my Tomko experience. Sonny wrote us about his high school shop class experience in Lamesa, Texas.

Sonny's freshman year was in a brand new high school building. One of the additions to the curriculum in the new building was shop. The shop teacher was rough and tough coach Martin, one of the football coaches. Sonny and the other students were all freshman boys except for two seniors who were assisting the coach with the class and receiving graduate credit. As the saying goes, "When the cat's away the mice will play."

The students started throwing small chunks of wood at each other in spite of the attempts of the seniors to persuade them to stop. But their effort was all in vain as the fight got worse and worse, and chunks of wood made it appear like a snow storm. At the very moment Coach Martin stepped in the door, a large chunk passed just below his nose. Instantly he ordered all 27 freshman boys to line up and bend over (only the two seniors were spared) and he went down the line setting each one on fire with his famous shop paddle. Coach Martin really understood how to adjust the attitude of the students.

Sonny wrote, "He was not only one of my favorite teachers in high school, but also one of my favorite coaches. I will never forget the time he and his five-year-old son came out of school late in the afternoon, walking west on North 14th Street. I was riding my Harley-Davidson motorcycle and I pulled up beside them and offered them a ride home. They got on with his son in between us and away we went flying to their home. That welded our friendship together!"

We often think of our high school memories with the phrase "Those were the days!" But when we recall those wooden paddles, not everything about those days was good!

II.

GROWING UP IN PUNGO

OUR HOUSE

I was born on July 11, 1933, in the living room of the house in Pungo where I grew up. Pungo is a small village in what was then Princess Anne County, but it is now part of the City of Virginia Beach. My sister Liz was seven years old when I was born, and my sister Reba was three. Liz remembers that when I was six months old, Joe Burroughs was brought to our house by his nanny to play with me. I had a little toy bus which Joe wanted to take home with him. Mother said that was all right and they could bring it back later. Joe and I have been good friends ever since.

Our house was a farmhouse located some distance from the road, which was the tradition in the 19th century when it was built. Later, Dad sold several lots to Will Dozier, who built houses close to the road for himself and for several other families. Mother thought our house ought to be moved close to the road like our neighbors' houses. We had a drainage problem, and water stood around the house after big rains. Mother argued that the ground near the road was much higher and water would drain off better, and after much pleading on her part Dad finally agreed to have the house moved in 1940. Dad hired the Baptist pastor to come with his 1939 Chevrolet to move the house. They jacked up the house and put telephone poles under it and rolled it on the poles. It was not a very good deal for the pastor because his clutch burned out, but they got the house to the designated spot.

❊

CHRISTMAS IN PUNGO

Christmas at our house was a very special time. For several years I led a worship service for my family before we could open our Christmas presents. The service included singing carols, reading appropriate scripture lessons, and my preaching a brief sermon. My sisters were not very happy about having to go through the worship service before we could open any presents, but they survived. They continue complaining about that to this day.

The first Christmas gift I remember was a pair of black rubber boots with a red band around the top. I was so happy with them that I wore them to bed.

I received a guitar for Christmas one year. It was a used guitar, but that didn't matter because I didn't know how to play it anyhow. My neighbor Billy Dozier also got a guitar, so he and I decided to put on shows for the neighborhood. His dad had a large tool house out back where we made the stage for our shows. We secured chairs for the audience to use. We even charged admission for the shows. Neither of us could play the guitar, but we sang with gusto cowboy songs that we had heard in the movies. The audience was very gracious even though they realized that our singing and playing were bad. After several performances our show business declined for lack of interest. We divided up our earnings, and that was the end of the shows.

SCHOOL DAYS

When I was six years old I started school in the new Creeds Elementary and High School, completed in time for the 1939-40 school year. There was a lot of sand on the school property, and many delivery trucks got stuck in the sand. We children helped push the trucks out. On one occasion I was helping push a pickup truck that had a cover on the back. My right thumb got hung between the body and the cover, and the driver did not realize it. He drove out of the driveway and turned left, throwing me into the ditch. Joe Batten, a high school student, saw what happened. He ran out, picked me up, and took me in to the teacher. After we discovered there were no broken bones and that I was all right, the teacher bawled me out for hanging onto the truck. We explained that I was helping push it out of the sand and my thumb got stuck between the body of the truck and the cover, and then she became sympathetic.

One time I was punished at school. During recess, I stayed in the classroom and climbed up on the high shelf of a coat closet. When the teacher came back to the room and discovered me on that shelf, she demanded that I come down, which of course I did immediately. She went to her desk, pulled out a ruler, and held my fingers while she beat the palm of my right hand. It was difficult for me to do any writing the rest of the day. I never climbed up on that shelf again.

VISITS FROM A CITY COUSIN

(As told by Shirley Whitehurst Brown)

Before building his little house in my family's back yard in Pungo, my great-uncle, "Uncle Oscar," lived with his wife Lizzie in an upstairs apartment above Meredith Drug Store at 17th Street and Pacific Avenue in Virginia Beach. My cousin Shirley Brown grew up in Norfolk, where she always had electricity, and she remembers visiting Uncle Oscar and being surprised to see that he did not have electricity in his apartment. He used a kerosene lamp for light, which was a new experience for her.

When Shirley was nine or ten years old, she and her father and mother, Uncle Vincent and Aunt Bertha, were driving to Pungo to visit my family when they had an accident on the section of Princess Anne Road we called the "five-mile stretch." A tire blew out, and the car went into a ditch and spun around and again backed into the ditch. All four fenders were curled. Her mother's cameo broach fell off and went out the window. A watermelon in the back seat was smashed so that there was watermelon all inside the car. Also the back seat came out and hit Shirley's back. Her dad worked hard to get the car out of the ditch, saying, "We've got to do it before the day changes to night." There was very little traffic on the road at that time, and somehow they were able to get on their way and there were no injuries.

Some time later Shirley came to our house to visit my sister Reba, and was surprised to find there was no running water or bathroom. She and Reba had to go out back to the wash house where clothes were washed in order to take their baths.

While the two of them were playing out back, they

picked a watermelon in the patch near Uncle Oscar's house and he said they could have it, but my mother scolded them and would not let them eat any of the watermelon. Uncle Oscar had a large needle which he used to make a net for fishing. It was the largest needle Shirley had ever seen.

Mrs. Luxford, across the road, had a white horse that she let Reba and Shirley ride. Unfortunately, Shirley fell off the horse one time into the ditch. Another "ditch" experience!

At another time, when she was in high school, Shirley came and spent a few days with Reba. One day she rode the school bus for the first time in her life, since in Norfolk she always walked to school, and attended Reba's classes with her at Oceana High School, which was quite a bit smaller than Maury High School in Norfolk. By that time we had a bathroom and running water in our house, which made it better for Shirley as well as for us.

CHILDHOOD FUN

Every Saturday, Dad bought each of us children a ten-cent bag of candy at a Pungo store. I tried to eat my candy very slowly so it would last several days. Two candies I remember especially that were always in the bag were Tootsie Rolls and Mary Janes. I particularly liked chocolate candy, and I still do.

As a child I did a bit of carpenter work. I ended up building two playhouses, one of which was attached to the wash house out back. As I recall, the roof of that playhouse was an old wooden door. Even though it did not last long, I did manage to pick some flowers, place them in a jar with water, and make it look like a home.

The other playhouse was under the giant pecan tree out back. That was a much larger endeavor, and it lasted much longer. My neighbor Billy Dozier helped me build it, using scrap lumber provided by his dad. One day our friend Snooky Mosley came to see my playhouse. He was quite impressed with what we had done. He said, "There is one more thing you need." "What is that?" I asked. "You need a sign," he said, and he wrote on a board, "No Treespassing!" I said, "Snooky, we've been working on the house for several days and not a single tree has passed." He was not impressed with my comment.

Another day, when four of us boys were playing behind Brock's Store, I found a $20.00 bill on the ground, picked it up and said excitedly, "Look what I found – a $20.00 bill!" Snooky grabbed it out of my hand and said, "I'll take it in the store and get it changed into four $5.00 bills, one for each of us." Since he was older and bigger than I, there was no way I could stop him. Later I thought that I should have kept quiet about what I had found.

Joe Burroughs, Billy Dozier and I often rode our bikes five miles to the home of Dempsey and Morris Vaughan. When we got there, we'd ask, "What are we going to play?" Dempsey would say, "Let's ride bicycles!" Our response was, "We've just done that. How about something else?" We'd play baseball or play in the barn loft. Another activity was riding the Vaughans' mule bareback, since no saddle was available. The mule's backbone bruised my tailbone, so the bicycle ride home was not as much fun as the ride there had been.

Joe had a pony named Smokey that the kids in the neighborhood were permitted to ride. Smokey loved to throw off his riders and come back and bite the thrown-off rider. One day I was riding him and sure enough he threw me off. Joe remembers hearing me yell, "My leg is broken, my leg is broken!" About that time I saw Smokey come running at me showing his teeth. It became obvious to those watching that my leg was not broken, because I got up and outran Smokey.

Another horse-riding fall happened in the pasture of Kermit Land, Jr., who lived across the road from Joe. Kermit's horse was beautiful and full of life. One day Kermit let me ride his horse while he watched. All of a sudden I fell off the horse. Kermit yelled, "Get back on him so he'll know you're not afraid of him." I did just that -- I mounted again and continued to ride him with no problem.

One day I said to my parents, "My friends have horses and I want one too." They responded, "We can't afford it. After all, you have two sisters and your friends don't." I thought to myself, "Couldn't we do something about that?" However, I was glad I had friends who would let me ride their horses, and that I had two sisters.

Walt, 3 years old, between his sisters
Reba (left) and Elizabeth (right)

III.

PUNGO

PEOPLE

GRACE SHERWOOD, WITCH OF PUNGO:

THE REST OF THE STORY

(As told by Manford Nosay)

Grace Sherwood, the Witch of Pungo, was described in *Pungo Tales Two: Some Old, Some New*, which also contains a picture of her house. A Pungo farmer's wife, she was accused by her neighbors of being a witch, was convicted in 1706 after surviving an ordeal called "witch ducking," and spent the next nine years in jail. Three hundred years later, in 2006, she was officially pardoned by Virginia Governor Tim Kaine. Here is the rest of the story, according to long-time Pungo resident Manford Nosay and others.

Grace Sherwood was buried on the property of Horace Malbone, according to what Manford was told by some people his age and older. However, Horace's son Rusty Malbone said he had heard that many times, but he was convinced that it is on the property next door which belongs to Ellen Lane Wadsworth. When I asked Ellen about it, she said that it is on her property, behind a small cluster of trees next to the road. But there is no tombstone noticeable. David Flanagan used to rent that farm and he never saw a marker, but a man once showed Ellen's late husband, George Wadsworth, a placard from the Courthouse showing the grave's location. Ellen suggested that possibly there never was a marker because so many people hated Grace.

According to Manford, Grace was a beautiful woman and other ladies were jealous of her. They said she was a witch, and they wanted her to be drowned so that they would look better and their husbands would stay home more. Whenever it rained, the farmers would say to their wives, "It's raining and I can't work today, so I'll go to Norfolk to buy some materials." But they didn't always come back with materials.

Manford's brother-in-law, Elwood Robinson, used to own property next to the farm of Grace Sherwood on Muddy Creek Road. When Manford was a kid, Elwood used to take him over to that house. No one was living in it and it was in bad shape, ready to fall down. It was a two-story house that had two chimneys on each end, with four fireplaces on the first floor and four on the second floor. It had clapboard siding which had never been painted. The chimneys are still standing, but you can't see them from the road because there are too many trees around them.

After talking with Manford, I decided to drive to the corner of Independence Boulevard and Witchduck Road, near the Virginia Beach Town Center, to take a picture of the statue that has been erected in honor of the Witch of Pungo. That photograph is below, and on the following page there is a facsimile of the words found on a plaque at the base of the statue.

THE TRIAL OF 1706

AT WITCHDUCK POINT 10AM JULY 10TH 1706 GRACE SHER-
WOOD, THE DAUGHTER OF A CARPENTER AND THE WIFE OF
A PLANTER IN THE COUNTY OF PRINCESS ANNE WAS AC-
CUSED BY NEIGHBORS OF WITCHCRAFT. GRACE WAS TRIED
IN THE SECOND PRINCESS ANNE COUNTY COURTHOUSE,
FOUND GUILTY AND CONSENTED TO THE TRADITIONAL
TRIAL BY WATER. GRACE WAS TIED CROSSBOUND AND
DROPPED INTO WATER ABOVE MAN'S DEPTH. IF SHE WERE
TO SINK AND DROWN SHE WAS INNOCENT AND COULD BE
BURIED ON HOLY GROUND. GRACE DID FLOAT, THUS WAS
GUILTY AS THE PURE WATER WAS CASTING OUT HER EVIL
SPIRIT. SHE WAS INCARCERATED IN THE LOCAL JAIL JUST
BEYOND THIS STATUE. AFTER HER RELEASE, GRACE PAID
THE BACK TAXES ON HER PROPERTY IN 1714, RETURNED TO
HER FARM AND WORKED THE LAND UNTIL HER DEATH AT
AGE 80 IN THE AUTUMN OF 1740. GRACE SHERWOOD, VIR-
GINIA'S ONLY CONVICTED WITCH. TRIED BY WATER, SHE
LAYS CLAIM TO WITCHDUCK ROAD, AND HER LEGEND LIVES
ON AS
"THE INFAMOUS WITCH OF PUNGO"

HENRY "BLIND" STONE

(As told by Manford Nosay)

Henry Stone, who was often called "Blind" Stone, lost the eyeballs from the sockets of his eyes and skin had grown over them so you couldn't see where the sockets were. He bought fish from Owen Gilbert, who did all of his fishing at Sandbridge Beach. Stone went down the road selling them. Since he was blind, he could not drive and so he had a driver to go with him.

People often tried to take advantage of Stone, but he knew how to tell how much money was given him. Sometimes a person would hand him a nickel and say it was a quarter and he would say, "I know that it's a nickel." He could even tell the value of paper money, and his driver was always watching and would help him. And in addition to money, he could tell what kind of fish there were. They could be spots, bluefish, butterfish, flounder, or croaker.

Stone bought ice at the Pungo Ice Plant, which was run by Charlie Dudley, and after getting his fish, his first stop was at the ice plant. The driver would go up on the high porch and get the ice while Stone remained in the car. On one occasion the driver stayed so long up there that Stone blew his horn. Shortly afterwards he blew it again, a little longer. The driver was icing the fish for him and also talking with Charlie Dudley.

Finally, when the driver opened the door, Stone said, "Dammit, can't you see that cloud coming up? It's gonna rain. We've got to go home." Charlie heard that and looked to the west and saw that there was a terrible storm on the way. He wondered how Stone knew that. Manford said, "Maybe there was some thunder and lightning."

Manford's mother and father bought fish from Stone, who could tell where his fish customers lived by the sound of their roosters crowing. He learned that each rooster's crow has a different sound. To let people know that he had come he would yell, "Fish man!" He had a big voice and people came running with pans in their hands. Sometimes the fish were so fresh they were still flapping. You could buy any kind of fish for 10 or 15 cents a pound. Stone made good money. He supported himself, and when he got older he drew Social Security and kept right on selling fish.

FRANK KELLAM

(As told by his son David Kellam and nephew Philip Kellam)

Frank owned and operated the Kellam and Eaton Hardware Store just across from the Princess Anne Courthouse. Sometimes I went to the store with my dad, and Frank seemed very pleased to see us. He usually gave Dad a discount, and I suspect he did that for many people.

What a delightful time for me to sit down with David and Philip. Here are some of the things they told me:

The store carried most anything – hardware, lumber, garden, plumbing, appliances, groceries -- and had a butcher who fed generations of workers on the Courthouse hill. People came from miles around to make their purchases. Frank's son David managed the lumber yard. All the mail for the Kellam families residing nearby had their mail delivered to the store. Frank was among the first persons in Princess Anne County to give credit, so that people could charge their bills and pay later.

In addition to running the store, Frank served as a mail carrier on the route that took him through Pungo Village. In *Pungo Tales Two: Some Old, Some New*, I remember mentioning that Ann Gregory and her sister Katie Flanagan as children used to wait on the fence for Frank to deliver their mail and he would give each of them a piece of chewing gum along with the mail. I wondered if the chewing gum was more important to them than the mail.

Frank was the 10th of 17 children: Hope, Fred, Mary, Floyd, Lillian, Alvah, James, Sidney, Herbert, Frank, Baby, Edwin, Thorogood, Richard, Robert, Harold, and Bill. Perhaps that is how he developed such a memory for names.

When customers came into the store, he graciously welcomed them and called them by name. He knew a great number of people in Princess Anne County. It was always a pleasure to shop there.

In the Nimmo United Methodist Cemetery, I saw a tombstone with the following inscription: "Mary Bateman Kellam – February 28, 1908 – December 26, 1985 and Frank Wallace Kellam – October 11, 1905 – December 25, 1994." I said to David, "After two December deaths, Christmas must have been a sad time for you after losing both of your parents during that season." He said, "Yes, for a long time it was very sad."

REV. JAKE MAST AND THE OYSTER

SUPPERS

Rev. Jacob W. "Jake" Mast was pastor of Charity United Methodist Church from 1945-49, when I was a boy. We young people liked the fact that he played ping-pong with us, and he was hard to beat. Another thing I remember in particular was his love for oyster suppers. Those suppers happened once a year and there was always a big crowd. It was a community event with good fellowship.

The Odd Fellows Lodge was across the road from the church, and the church was able to use the downstairs as a fellowship hall. There were many social events in that hall, such as baby showers, wedding receptions, etc. But of course, the greatest event was the oyster suppers with those delicious Chesapeake Bay oysters being cooked to perfection. The smell of those oysters cooking was noticeable before entering the hall. We children played outdoors, running among the many parked cars until we were called in to eat.

From 1971-77, part of the time I served as a pastor on the Lynchburg District, Jake was my District Superintendent. Whenever I saw him during those years, I would usually mention something about those oyster suppers, and his face would light up. He remembered his time at Charity Church with a great deal of happiness, especially those oyster suppers. After he retired in 1977, he took on the responsibility of serving as pastor of Bethlehem Church in the Moneta section of Bedford County. On one occasion he invited my family to an oyster supper at that church, remembering that I liked them as much as he did.

Jake died on April 26, 2006, and I went to his funeral. I had the opportunity to talk with his son, Jacob W. Mast, Jr.

He was happy that a member of the Whitehurst family from Charity Church had come to the service. I told him what good memories we had of his dad as our pastor, and that we especially liked the oyster suppers. I added that his dad had invited us to an oyster supper at Bethlehem Church when he was there. He smiled and said, "My dad was happy to have an oyster supper in all the churches he served after leaving Charity Church." I was not surprised to hear that!

DOUG BROWN

(As told by his widow, Joan Brown)

I was so impressed with Doug Brown every time I saw him that I wanted to get to know him better. He was such a pleasant person and was obviously a man with a deep faith in God. I would ask him, "Doug, how are you doing?" and with a big smile on his face he would respond, "Much better than I deserve!" That communicated to me that he was expressing gratitude to God for his many blessings. I decided that a good way to learn more about him was to interview Joan and include what she said about him in this book. Here are some memories Joan shared with me.

Doug was born in Norfolk General Hospital. He grew up in the Ghent section of Norfolk and graduated from Maury High School. He studied at Old Dominion University and became a civil engineer. He owned a heavy-duty construction business, and built bridges and culverts all over Hampton Roads and even as far away as Delaware. Doug oversaw the construction of two homes for his family, one in the Thomas Corner area and the other one in Alanton where they lived for 32 years. Later they moved to the Back Bay area where they had wanted to live for several years. Their house is on the water, so he could go fishing early Sunday morning and finish in time to go to Sunday School.

As a child, Doug had a heart murmur and was under a doctor's care for two years. When he was beginning to get better, he got out of bed a little bit too fast one morning and fell to the floor. His mother died when Doug was 15 years old, leaving his dad with the responsibility of raising him with the help of his aunt. In his early 20's he committed his life to Jesus Christ, and from then on he loved to lead people to the Lord. He was very active at Oak Grove Baptist Church where he served on many committees, taught Sunday School, was a Deacon for many years, and was a prayer warrior with Pastor Chuck Moseley. He led their three children to the Lord, as well as one granddaughter.

His son Doug Jr. said about him, "We all affectionately called our Dad and Granddaddy 'Popsie.' He always answered the phone by saying, 'YELLOW.' Popsie always greeted everybody with a smile and his signature handshake, which we called 'the Popsie roundhouse.' He loved to work in the yard. He told his granddaughter Nikki and daughter Patti that he was going to heaven first so he could create a beautiful garden that we could all enjoy when we arrive in heaven.

"He was very devoted to his grandchildren. He went out of his way to make certain he was there when they needed him. Any time the grandchildren did something special academically or athletically, he would take credit by stating to me and my sisters that that particular trait skipped a generation.

"Here are some of Popsie's favorite phrases: 'Never say you can't' . . . 'You can do anything you set your mind to do, with God's help' . . . 'If you start something, you need to finish it' . . . 'Never quit' . . . 'Why is there never enough time to do it right, but always enough time to do it over?' "

On Tuesday night, April 8, 2008, Doug got to see all his grandchildren. He even talked to his son who was in Portugal and somehow a button was pushed on the answering machine which caused that conversation to be recorded, and Joan has a tape recording of it. He had gone to the hospital for two minor tests early that morning, and Joan took him home that afternoon. He wanted to stop by Kentucky Fried Chicken to get some food so Joan would not have to cook that night. However, when it was supper time he didn't have any appetite, and by 8:30 he wanted to go to bed. When she said good night, he responded "goodbye," which was unusual because he never said goodbye to her.

The next morning, April 9th, his daughter Pam called to see how her dad was doing, and Joan said, "I don't know. He hasn't gotten up yet." That was strange, because he usually got up early. Finally, at 9:30 Joan went to the bedroom and called him, but there was no answer. When she touched him, he was cold and she realized he had died.

Later, Joan was reflecting on why Doug said "goodbye," and my wife Betty told her that originally "goodbye" meant "God Be With Ye!" It's almost like he knew that he was going to die and he was saying to Joan, "May God be with you!"

HORACE MALBONE:

JACK OF ALL TRADES AND MASTER OF MANY

(As told by his son, Rusty Malbone)

Horace was born on June 18, 1934, and died on April 2, 2011. He was a well-respected lifelong farmer and owner of a family-operated business in Pungo, Malbone Feed and Seed. He and his wife Helen had three sons: Dennis, Scott, and Rusty; and a daughter, Kirby.

Rusty said that one time there was a party in progress on the Garcia farm, where the Eagle's Nest housing development at the corner of Indian River Road and West Neck Road is presently located, when Horace and Rusty were called to come help with the birth of a calf. It was a breech birth, and the cow was running around with the calf hanging out. Horace pulled the dead calf out. A woman at the party asked Horace if he was going to give mouth-to-mouth resuscitation to the calf. Horace said, "No, but do you want to come over the fence and do it?" Her loud response was, "No!" He said, "Come over and have at it!" She did not take him up on that.

Rusty remembers hearing his dad tell about the times some of the neighborhood boys used to play ball on the Harold James property across the road. Sometimes after a rain the ground would be wet, but that was not a problem. Horace would pour gas or kerosene on the grass and burn it off and then they would play. In those days they made do with whatever was available.

John Brock had a blacksmith shop farther south on Princess Anne Road where Horace worked sometimes as a helper. He learned how to do welding as he watched John do it, and to work with metal. Those skills helped Horace later as he worked on the farm. At one time, John Brock's son Allan delivered newspapers, and on some occasions when Allan was out of town Horace did that for Allan. That meant 99 papers were delivered all the way from Pungo to Knott's Island, North Carolina. Those times were tough, and farming did not always provide enough income to make ends meet, so Horace had to do whatever he could to provide for the family. At times he worked with Kermit Land, who owned the Princess Anne Telephone Company. He helped to put up telephone poles, and once when he realized that a pole was falling he slid down the pole as fast as he could, which meant he got creosote-treated splinters on his hands and legs that stayed on him for a long time.

One winter Horace gathered up ice from West Neck Creek to bury behind his house and used it as a refrigerator to preserve meat. He and his wife Helen were good ice skaters, and when Back Bay froze over in 1977 they took advantage of that opportunity to go skating on the bay. Years later, in 1988, Horace took his granddaughter Tyler skating and was just as good a skater as ever, skating backwards to help her skate.

On December 13, 1983, their son Scott died in Middleburg, Ohio. Two weeks before Scott died, he called home to say that he was thinking about leaving his wife and coming back home. He was killed when the house trailer fell off its foundation and pinned his head to the ground. When Horace and his family went there, they found the trailer back on blocks and there was no evidence of blood. Horace and Helen stayed there a week or more to help out with the grandchildren Jason and Joshua.

Shortly after that I was visiting my parents in Pungo, and I happened to see Horace. He shared with me his sorrow at the death of his son Scott. He wanted to have Scott's body transferred to Pungo and be buried in the family plot at the Charity Church Cemetery, but it could not be arranged. I felt the deep double grief that Horace was going through.

Horace made a major contribution to the Virginia Beach 4-H Livestock Club by curing hams which were later sold by that organization. Actually, it was Helen who was in on that program from its beginning, and Horace continued it. When she started it, they cured only14 hams. The program has continued under the direction of Rusty and now they cure 268 hams. The profits of the annual auction of the hams go to the Horace and Helen Malbone Memorial Scholarship Fund.

Horace was always interested in helping people. A friend of his daughter Kirby recently told her that her dad was the reason he had finished high school. He had dropped out when he learned he had diabetes, which in those days was devastating news. Horace talked to him about the importance of getting his high school education, and he returned to school and graduated, thanks to Horace.

For many years, Rusty worked for the Ford Plant in Norfolk, while helping his dad with farming as much as he could. When the plant closed, Horace feared that Rusty would move away. Instead, Rusty decided to stay and farm with his dad. Rusty said, "The closing of the Ford Plant was the best thing that could have happened." He and Horace be-came much, much closer as they worked together. Naturally there were some differences of opinion as the "old school" and the "new school" worked together. But each one learned to appreciate their different approaches, and Horace told his fellow farmers to listen to what Rusty had to say about work-ing on combines.

The winter before Horace died, there was a snow-storm. Just as he had done in his childhood, he went out and gathered snow to make "snow cream." He said, "As long as I'm alive, we're going to eat snow cream!"

When Helen was near death, Horace said, "I know where she's going (meaning to heaven)." Jack Burroughs went with me to visit Horace and I reminded him what he had said about Helen. Then I asked him how it was between him and the Lord, and he said, "It's all right." That settled it.

❄

JACKIE WHITEHURST HERTZ

(As told by her daughter, Cheryl Hertz)

Jackie and I started first grade together at Creeds School in 1939, the first year the building was open. But after the sixth grade, several of us who lived in Pungo Village transferred to Oceana High School. Jackie had a good sense of humor, and I had fun kidding with her about that. She would say, "You abandoned us!" Or sometimes I would say to her, "Which one of us abandoned Creeds School?" She would point her finger at me and say, "You're the one who abandoned Creeds!" That continued to be a part of our conversations until the last time I saw her. People would ask her, "Are you from Pungo?" Her quick response would be, "No, I'm from Charity Neck!" I recently learned that her family did live in Pungo when she was a little girl. If I had known that before, I would have said to her, "If you had continued to live in Pungo, you could have gone to Oceana High School also."

One time I asked Jackie how she met her husband, Jim Hertz. When she was at Mary Washington College and Jim was a Marine at Quantico, she was at the reception desk when he came to see a girl. As it turned out, that girl was not there. So Jim asked Jackie if she would like to go out to eat. She said, "Yes, I always accept an invitation to go out to eat." (Her daughter Cheryl said Jackie told her, "If you've ever eaten college food, you'll understand why I went out with him.") The other girl lost out because Jim kept coming back and inviting Jackie to go out to eat. The rest is history!

Here are some of the memories Jackie's daughter Cheryl shared with me:

"Our parents gave my brother Jay and me a four-wheel-drive jeep when we were teenagers," Cheryl said, "and we spent a lot of time driving it on beaches. We drove all the way from Sandbridge Beach to Corolla in North Carolina and even to Nags Head. Jay and I have always been close, and that has continued throughout our lives. We decided to be the people our parents wanted us to be, which meant that we decided to drop our egos and say to people 'I love you' in honor of our parents and grandparents."

Jackie was non-judgmental and very accepting of people, no matter who they were. The way Jackie treated her mother was the way Cheryl wanted to treat Jackie. Jackie was Cheryl's model of how to live. When Jackie and Jim had a surprise 50th wedding anniversary at the Farm Bureau in 2005, barbeque was served -- the family tradition for special events -- and friends were asked to write love letters to them. One of the letters said, "If I were stranded on an island, I would want to be there with you two." There were many more expressions of love and appreciation.

Even though Jackie was kind and gentle, she could do whatever was necessary. Since their house was near Back Bay, they often saw snakes nearby, especially in the bay. In her childhood, Cheryl remembers being attacked by them occasionally. One time in particular she was in a boat by the shore, when all of a sudden the boat was attacked by cottonmouth snakes, which were the worst about attacking whenever someone got close to their nest. Jackie grabbed an oar and broke their backs and threw them ashore and chopped off their heads. For Cheryl, that was amazing to see. Jackie quickly said to her, "Don't try this!"

Cheryl remembers Jim as a strict father. She also describes herself as difficult to deal with in her growing-up days. She and Jim argued a lot. [I told Cheryl, "My father-in-law used to say that a child who was a problem or spoiled in the early days usually turns out to be a very fine adult, and I think that is what happened to you."] Cheryl eventually learned that Jim has a tender heart and is really concerned about people. He kept saying to Barbara Henley, a city councilwoman, that something needed to be done to keep older people in their homes rather than having to go into a nursing home. He really bugged her about that until he and Jackie heard about a program in Beacon Hill in the Back Bay section of Boston. (Since we have a Back Bay in our area, it just seemed to fit.) Booklets about it were ordered, and Barbara brought together a committee. One thing led to another, and today we have a wonderful Senior Resource Center which is making a major contribution to our community. Barbara said, "If it hadn't been for Jim and Jackie, we would have never had this center."

Jim made furnishings for the center, as he had done for Charity Church. He also became concerned about the narrow country roads in this area, and pushed for getting white lines on the sides of the roads to prevent people from going into the ditch.

When Cheryl graduated from college, she told Jackie that she wanted to move to Colorado. Of course Jackie preferred that Cheryl stay in Virginia, but she realized that Cheryl had to make her own decisions. She said to Cheryl, "You don't owe me anything. Just promise me that you will always have health insurance. If you get sick and don't have insurance, as your parent I'm not legally obligated to you, but I am morally obligated to you. I don't want to have to spend my retirement money on your health." Cheryl followed her mother's wish and got health insurance, even though in the early years when finances were not very good, she sometimes did not have enough money to buy good food. She told all her friends in Colorado (who affectionately call her ChaCha rather than Cheryl) what her mother had said.

I asked Cheryl if she was present the moment Jackie died. She said, "No. I knew my mother loved coffee, and enjoyed the aroma of brownies baking. I had made coffee in the bathroom near her bedroom so that she could smell it, and I was in the kitchen making brownies. The chocolate gave her permission. My husband Leslie was holding her hand and telling her that he would take care of me." What a nice tribute from a loving daughter and son-in-law!

PHILIP WAYNE MURDEN, SR.

(As told by his widow, Geraldine Brock Murden)

Phil was 81 years old when he died on February 6, 2013. I had the privilege of officiating for his graveside funeral on Saturday, February 9, a cold windy day, in the cemetery of Charity United Methodist Church. I shared that he and Gerri had been married for 56½ years and they had lived on a boat since 2002. My unplanned statement was that they had to have a good marriage to live that long together on a boat. I have known Phil and Gerri basically all my life.

Here are some of the memories Gerri shared with me:

Phil had a boat before they got married. He sold the boat to buy the engagement and wedding rings in preparation for their marriage. He soon was able to buy another boat which he used for fishing, and of course he loved to do hunting whenever he could. Throughout their life together they had many different boats. They would buy one in bad condition and refurbish it, and that was done many times. They bought one boat in Miami and brought it back to Virginia Beach. In their remodeling of boats, they often put wood paneling in them. Gerri enjoyed boats as much as Phil did. She even helped him to remodel boats they bought. They did all of that with much love.

When Phil was young, he was out with his father and he got too close to a beehive. The bees attacked Phil and stung him over much of his body. Everybody thought he was going to die. From then on he stayed clear of bees. One time while he was steering their boat, a bee got inside the boat while it was moving, and he immediately left the steering wheel and went below to get away from the bee. Fortunately, Gerri was nearby and could take over the steering. She knew how to run their boats. If she had not been there, who knows what would have happened to the boat, passengers and all.

Sometimes when the water was rough, he'd go down inside the boat to make certain everything was in order and Gerri would take over the navigating. However, there was a time when she got so seasick that she lost her voice for three days. Phil loved to kid her and laugh about how much he enjoyed those three days of complete silence.

Prior to moving permanently to the boat in 2002, they spent many summers and other times on the boat. Their two sons Wayne and Michael liked living on the boat as much as their parents did. When they were docked at Pungo Ferry Marina, there were a lot of summer activities available. There was a ski ramp, and the two boys took skiing lessons. They spent a lot of time skiing on the waters of North Landing River, being pulled by a fishing boat. Wayne continues to love boats and what he has now is a racing boat. Even though Wayne knows a lot of details about the boat where his parents were living at West Neck Marina, Phil said there were a few details he wanted to tell Wayne about, but he never got it done.

Phil's mother Ruby Murden lived until she was almost 106 years old. Her mind was sharp until just before her death in 2001. She took very good care of Phil's brother Forest who had Down Syndrome. He was very intelligent and had an amazing memory; for example, he never forgot names of people he met. Since Ruby never learned how to drive, she did not take Forest places. She was very kind to everyone and she especially had a lot of patience with Forest. Gerri remembers there were never unkind words between Ruby and herself. With a smile, Gerri added, "Although I may have tried her patience sometimes!" After her death, Forest ended up living with Phil and Gerri, which meant that they took him places with them and he got to see things he had not been able to see before.

Gerri remembers two funny stories about Forest. One was when she and Phil took Forest to a condo in Williamsburg. Forest had never seen a Jacuzzi before. They let him go in it, and he did not want to get out. He enjoyed it so much that when he got home after being in the Jacuzzi he said to Phil and Gerri, "I know what I want Santa Claus to bring me for Christmas – a Jacuzzi!" Their response was, "That would not be possible. Where would we put it?" That was no problem at all for Forest. His quick response was, "We can put it in the middle of the living room!" (They were still living in their house at that time.)

The second one was when Phil and Gerri took Forest to Home Depot. Since he had not been there before, he was amazed at all the many things he saw there. If Gerri had not taken him by the hand, he would have wanted to see every single item in the whole store. It would have taken many days for him to see it all.

Forest died from pneumonia in 2002. After that Phil and Gerri moved permanently to the boat. Throughout their marriage it was agreed that neither one would leave. Instead, they would stay together and solve any problems. Sometimes they stayed up very late doing the solving because they knew that if one of them left, he or she could not come back. Another decision was that in their home God's name would not be taken in vain. Gerri remembers that one time she did take God's name in vain, and Phil firmly reminded her that if she did that again their marriage would be over. The end result was 56½ years of a good happy marriage.

❄

REV. JOHN W. HAYNES: LED BY THE SPIRIT

During the six Sunday nights of Lent, several churches in the greater Pungo area share Sunday night services, meeting in a different church each time. On February 17, 2013, our first Lenten service was at Asbury United Methodist Church. At the end of the service, it was announced that Pastor John would be leaving the church in June after being the pastor of Asbury since 1990. I decided to include his story in Pungo Tales Three. On Sunday afternoon, March 10, we had lunch with Pastor John in our home. Below are some things Betty and I learned about his life.

Pastor Haynes said that his spiritual journey into the ministry began on the 29th of July, 1924, in Pittsburg, Pennsylvania, when he was born to a childless couple, Elijah and Clara Haynes. He was raised in the Methodist Church and participated in the Sunday School and youth activities until he graduated from high school. The church leaders encouraged him to assume greater responsibilities in the church program because of his willing attitude. He also participated in YMCA activities where he developed a desire to help people.

In July 1943, Pastor John answered the call from Uncle Sam; he went straight from high school into the United States Army. During his tour of service for his country he met and married Ethel Hatcher on November 9, 1946, and they remained in this union for 52 years. They were blessed with two children, Steven and Lisa. Steven was a rambunctious child and in order to keep him in Sunday School, his father started teaching classes. As Steven was promoted, John was also promoted. He started working with the Cub Scouts and then the Boy Scouts, even serving on the Scout Committee, and rejoiced when his son became an Eagle Scout. Steven graduated from Norfolk State University in 1978 and moved to San Diego, California. His passion for helping youth, mixed with his love of sports, led to his creating a non-profit organization named Athletes for Education (AFE), which is still functioning today.

After Steven's untimely death on February 18, 2011, Pastor John wrote the following tribute to his son: "He lived his life his way. When you are doing things your way for the benefit of others, you are doing it God's way and for the glory of God."

John also helped with the Babe Ruth League. God blessed him with the opportunity to teach a Bible study class to Japanese nationals through an interpreter when he was stationed in Japan. He also taught Bible study in Germany, and his daughter Lisa was his companion. While the adults were studying, Lisa played with the friends she had made in Germany. This became one of their father and daughter moments. She also enjoyed helping with Sunday School and the youth programs. Lisa received her associate degree in early childhood education and is now working for Norfolk Public Schools.

John had made a promise to God that when he and his wife had children, they would never see him drink or smoke, so he would go directly home after work (to keep his son and daughter occupied) instead of going to happy hour as many did. He had also made a commitment that anywhere they were stationed they would be actively involved in the church.

On June 23, 2001, after the death of his first wife, God blessed Pastor John with another helpmate, Shirley William, and her four daughters who accepted him as their Pop.

John started taking college classes when he was stationed in Alaska and added more college credits while stationed in Texas. In August 1973 after his retirement from the military as a First Sergeant, where he was responsible for the health, welfare, and morale of the enlisted personnel in his squadron, he entered Virginia Wesleyan College in Norfolk, Virginia, as a full-time student, using his GI Bill. In September 1977 he entered Virginia Union Seminary in Richmond, Virginia, and received his Master of Divinity in 1980.

Dr. Carl Hailey, Portsmouth District Superintendent, appointed Pastor John to his first church, Elm Avenue United Methodist Church in Portsmouth, Virginia. The church has been renamed Martin Luther King United Methodist Church. His most challenging yet rewarding assignment was at Galloway United Methodist Church in Falls Church, Virginia, where he helped the congregation to plan, organize, and direct the building of a new sanctuary. His labor of love was rewarded when the church named the educational wing in his honor.

Later, Pastor John wrote the following postscript to our conversation:

"During my years at Asbury United Methodist Church my spiritual development matured as God awarded me my PHD (Praise, Honor, and Devotion)," Pastor John said. "Leaving Asbury UMC, I'm reminded of St. Paul's words, 'for I have fought the good fight and kept the faith.' I'm ready for God's next assignment. I leave with a smile on my face, joy in my heart, and peace in my soul, being led by God's spirit.

"Food for Thought – I will always remember the love and the kindness that the Asbury congregation has given to me. They were most supportive of my ministry when they realized that I was the caretaker for my wife and raising two grandboys. These wonderful people showed compassion that was beyond my expectation. Thank You!"

THE LIFE OF VELMA STRADLING

CASON MARTIN

When I called and explained my desire to interview Velma and tell about her life, she offered to give me a copy of a document she had written some years ago. Here are some thoughts I have gleaned from that paper:

Velma was born in Fletcher, North Carolina, on December 18, 1932 – a cold, windy night with six inches of snow on the ground. When her mother, Ethel Unice Henderson Stradling, started labor, her father, Earl Leroy Stradling, borrowed a horse from a neighbor and went to get the doctor. By the light of a full moon, he walked, leading the horse with the doctor riding. It must have been a terrible trip, but the doctor arrived at their house in time to deliver the new baby.

The first home Velma remembers was in Flat Rock, North Carolina. It had three rooms – two bedrooms and a great room. Baths were in the wash tub, with water heated on a wood stove. Those were hard times, and Velma's father, who worked in electrical construction, was unable to find work until he got a job as a guard on a convict road gang.

Next the family moved to Black Mountain, North Carolina, a nice small town that provided a safe place to play and roller skate in the street. There were mountains to climb and trains to watch and a hosiery mill with big glass windows where the children could watch some of the manufacturing process. Huge plywood boxes that sold for 25 cents each made wonderful playhouses. The children cut windows in the boxes and hung curtains.

With no nearby girls to play with, Velma's best friend was Ralph, a boy her age who lived next door. They explored the area, climbed trees, and built things. With his 25-cent-a-week allowance he often treated Velma to the movies, which cost 10 cents each, and then they shared five cents' worth of hard candy or liquorish sticks. Velma's family went to a Baptist church. She was impressed by a woman, draped in a long white robe, singing "The Old Rugged Cross."

When World War II came along the family moved to Princess Anne County, Virginia (now a part of the City of Virginia Beach). They bought a farm on Charity Neck Road. Blackout shades covered all the windows, and searchlights lit up the skies, looking for enemy planes. Everyone saved aluminum for the war effort – even gum wrappers.

One of Velma's new friends was a neighbor, "Miss" Annie Whitehurst, who often took Velma to Charity Church with her. When Velma was eight years old she was baptized and joined Charity Church. She went to Creeds School on the big yellow school bus, and was an AAA school patrolman. This made her eligible for a trip to Washington, D.C. Velma felt very important, marching down Pennsylvania Avenue.

At the beginning of her junior year in high school, Velma met John Early Cason, who had just returned from a year in Europe with the United States Army. He looked handsome in his uniform, and owned a speed boat and an airplane! He had noticed Velma in the choir at Charity Church and asked his mother, Mary Garnett Cason, to ask her if she would like to meet him. She said yes. She enjoyed going flying with John Early, and after dating for two years they were married on December 30, 1950.

The newlyweds moved into the house that John Early grew up in. The original two-story part was built in the early 1800's. A big barn with a hay loft was torn down in 1956. A piece taken from the eaves, with the building date on it, is all that remains and is now on Velma's mantel.

In the fall, Velma's family and their Princess Anne County neighbors waited anxiously for the spot (a kind of fish that abounds in this area) to "run" so they could get their supply of spot to salt down for the winter. Once the spot were secured, they were washed, then scaled, the heads cut off and the fish split down the back. After another washing, they were placed in a tub of salted ice water for 30 minutes, drained, and packed in a clean "fish crock," with a layer of salt between each layer of fish. After a week, they took the fish out of the crock to make sure they were not stuck together. Then they repacked them and added brine to cover the fish. The brine was made by dissolving salt in water until it would float a fresh egg. The fish cured in about a month. The "salt spot" needed to be soaked in fresh water overnight before being boiled and served with pepper vinegar.

Years later, after John Early Cason's death, Velma met a widower, Jerry Martin, at the Princess Anne Recreation Center. They found they had many similar interests, fell in love, and were married. They are very devoted to one another and are well known for their service to the community.

Jerry is a devout Catholic, and Velma remains faithful to Charity United Methodist Church. They attend Mass together on Saturdays and go to Charity Church on Sundays. One Sunday, when their Sunday School teacher asked the class, "What do you want to have written on your tombstone?" several people gave their answers, and then Jerry spoke up. He said, "I want mine to say, 'He was the only Catholic in the Back Bay area to have his own key to Charity United Methodist Church.'" However, they later installed new doors and locks, and Jerry's key no longer works.

❄

IV.

PUNGO PETS

DOPEY AND BUSTER

One Sunday afternoon during my childhood, as we were driving home from church, I saw a woman and her daughter walking down the road carrying a puppy. They walked up to our house and brought the yellow pup, part collie and part hound dog, to me. I couldn't believe it – I would have my own dog!

Dad asked, "What name do you want to give him?" I had just seen the movie, "Snow White and the Seven Dwarfs," and chose the name "Dopey," not realizing that Dopey was a negative name; it was just one I liked. Dopey was a friendly, good-natured dog, and we grew up together.

Dad's coon dog Buster was black and white and about the same size as Dopey. When he treed a coon, Dad could tell by his bark that he had found one, and would take his flashlight and a gun to kill the coon. Often I went along to hold the light so he could do the shooting. Dad usually killed the coon with one shot. Then he'd bring it to the back yard, skin it, save the skin to sell, and cook the coon the next day.

THE CAT AND THE ROOSTER

(As told by Joe Burroughs)

Behind the house of Joe's parents, Fred and Malvine Burroughs, there was a high picket fence, along with a stable where the horses and ponies slept, a big barn where they kept corn and sometimes hay, and a section where there were chickens.

Joe tells the following story:

There once was a cat at the Burroughs farm who had many kittens in the barnyard where the chickens were kept. For some unknown reason, the mother cat left the farm. She took all of the baby kittens with her, except one. The kitten was left to grow up in the yard with the chickens, and the chickens paid no attention to him. With no other cats around, the kitten apparently considered himself to be a chicken.

Everything went smoothly until the kitten fell in love with the Rhode Island Red rooster. He began to follow the rooster around the barnyard, rubbing up against him and wrapping his tail around the rooster's neck. The rooster was not amused, and indeed he tried to get away from the kitten's affection. It got to the place that the rooster began to attack the kitten by picking at him. The kitten's love was so deep that he did not use his claws to retaliate. We could not say this story ended with the phrase "They lived happily ever after!"

RAVEN, EVERYONE'S FRIEND

(As told by Phyllis Dowdy)

Some years ago, my parents' next-door neighbors, Fitzhugh and Phyllis Dowdy, had a beautiful flat-coated retriever named Raven – shiny black, with wavy hair on his back. In those days animals were free to run loose, and Raven was known to everyone in the neighborhood. Because he was such a friendly dog, he was loved by all.

One of Raven's favorite places was the 7-11 store next door to the Whitehursts and two doors down from the Dowdys. He would spend a part of each day sitting on the curb in front of the entrance to the store. Phyllis told the manager one day, "I'm sorry Raven is such a bother, sitting in front of the doors every day." The manager replied, "Oh, that's perfectly all right. We love Raven, and we feel so safe when he's here greeting the people." Phyllis thought to herself, "If a burglar came to our house, Raven would probably let him in and hold the flashlight for him."

Every Christmas, Raven was allowed into the house, and family members would help him open his presents. One Christmas after his gift – a brush – was opened, he put it in his mouth and carried it around the room, showing it proudly to each person in turn.

Unlike many dogs, Raven loved to go to the veterinarian. One day he had a 2:30 appointment at the veterinarian's office across the road in the Pungo Square shopping center. Phyllis called earlier that day to ask about the appointment, and the receptionist said, "Oh, you don't need to bring him in. He's already been here, and we've taken care of him." Raven had taken it upon himself to cross the road and wait in front of the office to be let in for his appointment!

Raven died peacefully in his nice warm doghouse on a New Year's Eve. When the Dowdys' son Jason came in just after midnight from being out with his friends, he took Raven his good-night bone, but noticed that Raven did not move to eat the bone as he usually did. Jason had to break the sad news to the family that their beloved dog had died. They went out to the back yard, and at 2:00 a.m. they were digging a very big hole in which to bury him, hoping the police would not drive by and stop to ask what they were doing.

Raven is missed by many of us who knew him, but the stories about him live on.

❋

AN OTTER NAMED PUNGO

Even though he did not live in Pungo, an otter who resided at the Virginia Aquarium & Marine Science Center in Virginia Beach, not far from Pungo, was given the name "Pungo" when he arrived at the aquarium in 1996 from a facility in Louisiana.

After his death from cancer at age 18, a beautiful photo of Pungo, the oldest remaining otter in the North American River Otter exhibit, was published at the top of page one in the Hampton Roads section of The Virginian-Pilot, along with the full story of his life and death on page two.

According to the article, Pungo was one of the first otters acquired by the Aquarium. Pungo, Willoughby, and Rudee arrived together to join Tango and Cash, who had come from a facility that rehabilitated captured wild animals. [Pungo's companions Willoughby and Rudee were named for two other locations in the cities of Norfolk and Virginia Beach.] Pungo was the last survivor of the original five otters. May he rest in peace.

❋

THE WORLD WIDE WEBBY

(By Sarah Burke)

On Friday mornings the Senior Resource Center hosts "Writing With Bob," when Bob Danner meets with persons who are interested in learning more about writing. They share what they have written and receive feedback from others present. One Friday, Sarah Burke brought this beautiful story about a beloved pet named Webby:

"When I first saw him I thought he was the cutest thing I had ever laid eyes on. He was about 12 weeks old, big dark eyes, and the prettiest red hair I had ever seen. His feet were bandaged and made to look like he was wearing Nikes due to work with a black marker. The girls carried him EVERYWHERE. His feet never hit the floor. This dog was spoiled rotten. He was born with webbed feet. The breeder wanted to put him down because he made the litter look bad. My friend Sharon, who ran the local Doberman Rescue, took him to our veterinarian. She said that because the pads of his feet were separate, she thought she could make his feet more usable and that's what she did. They weren't perfect but workable.

"I fell madly, deeply, and totally in love with him. The vet had named him WEBster due to his WEBbed feet and we thought it appropriate so we let it stand. It wasn't long before my husband fell for him, too. At night we put him in the kennel. He would cry and whine. I called Sharon and she said to leave him there and eventually he would be quiet. It takes time to train a puppy. The following day I called Sharon and said 'Guess What? He was quiet all night.' She said 'GREAT!...........wait a minute, Sarah. Where did he sleep?' 'UM........well.............in our bed with us.' And that's where he slept for the rest of his life.

"Everyone loved this dog. He was so sweet, loveable, and such a big baby one couldn't help but love him. I don't think this dog had a vicious bone in his body. Sharon said not to underestimate a Doberman, but this dog was different. I said to him, 'Who do you think you are? You give Dobermans a bad name! Dobermans are supposed to be vicious, mean, scary. You, my sweet, are a WUSS.'

"When he went outside he hated to go out alone. He always wanted company. If he wanted to come in, he would whine and whine, not bark. He always had stuffed toys. They were called his babies. He would NEVER go outside without one. If I said 'Go get your baby,' he would find where he left it and pick it up to bring it in. He was so funny. Webster was an 80-pound Doberman who thought he was a puppy. This big lummox actually sat in my lap. He loved to sit in my lap with his top part over the arm of the chair onto the sofa arm. His bottom half was actually on the attached bottom part of the recliner. It was so funny to see this huge dog sitting like a puppy in my lap. Talk about identity crisis!

"We raised him from a pup, and had the pleasure of his company for more than 10 years. Then he got bone cancer in his left hind leg. I asked the girls at the vet's office if they would be with him when 'it was time.' We just couldn't be there. It was too difficult. They assured me they would. When the day came that Webby couldn't stand any more my son and my husband put him in the car and took him to the vet. The girls stayed as promised. They all did a group hug with my husband and let him cry.

"I received a card from all of them about a week later. The vet expressed how grateful she was to have known him, what a special boy he was, and that she was proud to know we trusted her with our baby. It was a beautiful expression of love. She said he went peacefully after they laid him on the floor and fed him a BAZILLION Christmas tree cookies. I hope he knew just how much he was loved and how much we will miss him. The vet said it was the right time. I would never want him to be in constant pain, so that was good to know.

"It has just been two weeks. It seems like forever. I know it will get easier, but we will never ever forget him. I carry pictures of him and have some around the house. He was so special. A poor excuse for a Doberman but a really great dog. I know my baby will be there to greet me when I die. I hope he understood that we couldn't let him suffer. We did what we thought was best for him, not us.

"Until we meet again my love,

"Sarah Burke aka Momma."

V.

PUNGO PLACES

WHERE IS PUNGO?

I came across an article from the Norfolk Journal, March 15, 1870, with the headline "Where is Pungo?" It stated: "It is a notorious fact that the precise locality of this place, or district, or whatever, has never been determined. No man admits he was born in Pungo, but somewhere in the neighborhood. There is the story of a Norfolk man who promised a pair of boots to a Pungo native. One man said he was, but then wouldn't take the boots, because he was only born on the edge of Pungo. We can't tell why people disown one of the finest districts in Virginia. No part of the state is more naturally fertile, etc., but we have never found a man who confesses to be born in, or lived in, Pungo."

A follow-up quotation from the Norfolk Journal on April 23, 1870, said, "In response...we heard from a man recently who said he was from Pungo and didn't care who knew it."

At a Homecoming at Randolph-Macon College some years ago, one fellow looked at me and said with a surprised expression, "Walt Whitehurst, from Pungo, Virginia!" I quickly asked him, "How did you know I'm from Pungo?" He replied, "You're the only person I ever met from Pungo." That reminded me of the time when a classmate, hearing that I was from Pungo, asked me how many people lived in Pungo. I replied, "One hundred twenty-five." He asked, "Thousand?" and I responded, "No – people."

I'm proud to be living on the property where I was born and raised in Pungo. In Virginia, I've lived in Ashland, Williamsburg, Shawsville, Virginia Beach, Annandale, Rustburg, Bedford, Hopewell, and Richmond. I've also lived in Durham and Lake Junaluska, North Carolina; Santiago, Puerto Montt, and Temuco, Chile; and Atlanta, Georgia. And

I have visited many other countries. But Pungo has always been home. I retired in Pungo, and I'm proud to be from Pungo.

An article by Linda McNatt in the Beacon, a "Princess Anne" supplement to The Virginian-Pilot newspaper, on September 27, 2012, was about a Virginia Beach extension agent. (The City of Virginia Beach has a Department of Agriculture, with extension agents, thanks to the rural nature of the Pungo area.) The article included this statement: "He said he's in love with Pungo. What's not to like about a man in love with Pungo?"

Recently, on our way to Richmond, Betty and I went into a Rest Stop on I-64 West. When we came out of the restroom, there was a man staring at the little plate on top of my front license plate that says "Pungo, VA," with a strawberry painted between "Pungo" and "VA." The man asked, "Where in the hell is Pungo, VA?" I told him that my friend Joe Burroughs says it is the capital of Virginia Beach. Later, it occurred to me that I should have said, "The correct question is, where in heaven is Pungo?"

A few years ago, my wife Betty and I were on a Christmas cruise where I served as chaplain. The ship had a huge Christmas tree in the center and there was a Christmas Tree Lighting one night. The passengers were gathered around the tree singing Christmas carols. When we finished, a man who was standing in front of us turned and said, "You two must have sung in a church choir somewhere." I said, "Yes, we have sung in several church choirs." His next question was, "Where do you live?" When I said "Virginia Beach, Virginia," his quick response was, "The only place I know in Virginia Beach is Pungo." Then he explained that he had a business partner in Pungo. Maybe Pungo is better known than we thought!

THE PUNGO FISH HOUSE

In my first book, *Pungo Tales*, I told about what a joy it was for me to go fishing with my dad. He knew when the wind was blowing just right, when the fish would be biting, and what type of bait to have. He generally came home with fish. Sometimes when he did not catch anything at Sandbridge Beach, he would stop at Belanga Fish Company on Sandbridge Road and buy some. If Mother asked him if he brought home any fish, he would say yes, without mentioning that he had bought the fish he brought.

It was a sad day when he was no longer able to go fishing. But the sadness did not last long, because he started buying fish at Pungo Fish House. Dad and owner Robert Whitehurst became close friends until Dad's death in April 1985. Robert soon learned what kind of fish Dad liked. Whenever Dad wanted to buy fish, he'd call Pungo Fish House and ask, "Robert, what kind of fish do you have?" Dad would tell him which ones and how many he wanted, and then drive there to pick them up. Sometimes Robert would say, "Mr. Whitehurst, I'm sorry not to have anything now that you like, but I'll have some later. I'll call you when they get here." Later the phone call would come saying Dad's favorite fish had arrived.

Years later, when Dad could no longer drive, he continued to call Robert and ask what kind of fish was available, and Robert would see that Dad's fish were delivered to the house. That was good service, and we were grateful to Robert. We often commented that Dad lived to be 89 years old, partly because he ate a lot of fish.

The Pungo Fish House was started by Robert's grandfather, Levy Whitehurst. In the Charity Church cemetery, Levy's tombstone has a fish design on his portion, and on his wife Mildred's there is a mailbox design because for many years she was a mail carrier. When Levy retired, his son Clark Whitehurst, Robert's father, retired as a Virginia Beach police officer and took over the business. When Clark retired from running the Fish House, Robert continued the business. Three generations of that family have faithfully provided fish and crabs for people of the greater Pungo area. That represents a powerfully large amount of fish and crabs caught and bought.

Tombstone of Levy Whitehurst, founder of Pungo
Fish House, and his wife Mildred.

A HISTORY OF KNOTTS ISLAND

1902 to 1912

(Handwritten by H. B. Ansell)

Although Knotts Island is not in Pungo and indeed not in Virginia, there is a longtime relationship between the two areas. Pungo had English settlers in the 1600's, and Knotts Island by the 1700's. When I was at Creeds Elementary School, there were students from Knotts Island. Also, many people who live on the island work in Virginia and some drive through Pungo on their way to work and do their shopping in the Pungo area.

Nellie Leonardson found the following document as she was processing an estate.

"If you will look at the map of North Carolina, you will find Currituck County covers the northeast portion of the map and you will see a square part of land as if it was belched forth from the state of Virginia. Knotts Island covers part. It is one mile wide and seven and one half miles long with five miles in North Carolina and the remainder in Virginia.

"The island is famous for its apples, peaches, cherries, and many other fruits such as pears and figs. In past days in orchards and yards there were plenty for everyone and they were free for those who would help themselves.

"When the writer was a small boy, there were many startling yarns told of the ups and downs of the first settlers, such as contending with Indians, bears, wolves, wildcats and numerous reptiles. The first white settlers emigrated from London and Liverpool. They brought historical tales about

London Bridge that spans the River Thames. The game, London Bridge is falling down, came from them. It was said that when the husbands were away and the families were alone, the wolves would appear at their homes, then the doors would stay locked. Wild turkeys and Indians were plentiful on the island. When the white man hunted the turkeys, the Indians would hide in hollow trees and gobble, and when the white men approached the Indians would scalp them. Snakes represented a danger also. A certain man built a new log cabin, and the fireplace was built over a den of snakes. The family left a fire in the fireplace overnight, and the next morning the whole family was dead and the snakes were a foot deep in the house.

"The first settlers had to undergo some hardships, but they had plenty to eat. There were fish, oysters, turkeys, ducks, geese, and other birds. They raised corn and sweet potatoes and all they lacked was bread.

"During the Revolution there were on this island many short-straw pines so thick you could hardly see through them. The English in that war could not get their ships through Currituck Inlet, but would come through with yawls and ransack the island, taking and destroying everything. In order to save their property, the people put their beds and valuables in the thickets to save them. Eventually it was decided to fight the enemy. The American militia that was left on the island was ordered out. So down to the south end of the island they went. They were placed near the shore where the yawls usually came in. When the English spied the militia, they stopped and made all kinds of vulgar language and gestures and came no closer. One man fired and hit one of the British and they moved out."

❈

PUNGO CHURCHES

The Pungo community is blessed with churches of various denominations, which work together in a spirit of fellowship and mutual respect. Many of them participate in joint activities, including the annual series of Sunday night Lenten services and the Fifth Sunday "Singspirations." These activities take place in different churches, with pastors taking turns preaching for the Lenten services and musical groups from various churches performing at each of the Singspirations. The participating churches are listed below, with a brief statement about each one.

Asbury United Methodist Church

The only predominantly African American United Methodist Church in Virginia Beach, Asbury Church is a vital part of the Pungo community. Because it is special in many ways, the next "tale" is a history of that church.

Back Bay Christian Assembly of God

Back Bay Assembly recently celebrated 25 years of ministry to the community. The worship services I have attended there have been inspiring, and the list of missionaries supported by the church is most impressive, both in number and in geographical distribution. It is a congregation that provides vital worship, offers service to the community, and supports mission throughout the world.

Bethel United Methodist Church

Bethel Church was one of 19 churches on the Princess Anne Circuit when it was established in 1846, in the days of the circuit riding preachers. Little by little the circuit was divided – first into a circuit of eight churches, then five, four, and two. It became a station church when Beech Grove Church closed a few years ago. Its present building was constructed in 1946 after an earlier building burned in 1944.

Charity United Methodist Church

My home church has a sign out front that says "Charity United Methodist Church – Serving Christ & the Community Since 1789." Its origins, however, stem from the Church of England's Pungo chapels established in lower Princess Anne County beginning in the 1600's. The present church building was built in 1942 to replace the third building, built in 1901, which burned to the ground in 1941. Several additions have been made to the original building.

Charity Church is well known in the community for its fine pre-school and for its food pantry, as well as an outstanding youth program. "Grace" praise band plays each Sunday for the 8:30 praise service and the Chancel Choir sings for the 11:00 service. A new feature is the "Lute Society," consisting of ukulele players and guitarists who accompany the choir and congregation from time to time.

Creeds Church of Christ

In addition to its programs for children, youth, and young adults, Creeds Church of Christ sponsors an annual Senior Citizens Dinner each August for all seniors who wish to attend, with special invitations sent to an extensive mailing list. The meal is always delicious, the fellowship is great, and the program features special presentations by a variety of people and groups, and the church's praise band includes "The Pungo Song" in its repertoire.

According to the church website, "There are three basic practices that make us a church family. These practices are: Service to the Community, Fellowship with Each Other, and Teaching God's Word."

Nimmo United Methodist Church

The "Nimmo Meeting House," built in 1791, is the oldest surviving United Methodist Church building in continuous use in Virginia. Its name came from Anne Nimmo, who sold the church one acre of her land for five shillings. It is made of white clapboard, with plastered walls, and has colonial box pews with doors that open into each box. About 1840, a balcony was added as a slave gallery. Church records show that in 1846, Nimmo had 170 white members and 42 "colored members." During the Civil War, Nimmo Church was used to house Federal troops and as a Federal hospital.

Nimmo Church continues to have a vital congregation, reaching out to the community in many ways including a United Methodist Men's Christmas tree sale and a community garden each summer on church property.

Oak Grove Baptist Church

Oak Grove Church is the oldest Baptist church in the state of Virginia, established in 1762. It is a Southern Baptist Church and a member of the Baptist General Association of Virginia and the Norfolk Area Baptist Association. Before its first building was erected, Baptists congregated in an oak grove – hence its name – or went to Shiloh Baptist Church in Camden County, North Carolina, its mother church. Later, Oak Grove gave birth to five other local Baptist churches: Blackwater, 1774; London Bridge, 1784; St. John's, 1853; Piney Grove, 1870; and Knotts Island, 1876.

Saint Luke's United Methodist Church

Although not located in the Pungo area, Saint Luke's Church participates in Pungo activities. The church was started in August 1973 and officially chartered on Pentecost Sunday, June 2, 1974. It is in the Green Run area of Virginia Beach, not far from Pungo. The site on which is it located was once a part of the Rockefeller family holdings. The congregation, which met in the Green Run Clubhouse until the building was completed in 1979, is a multicultural congregation that thrives on vital worship and community outreach.

Sandbridge Community Chapel United Methodist Church

Sandbridge had its beginnings as a chapel, open only on Sundays, with a house where United Methodist pastors and their families could spend a week's vacation at the beach provided they would lead the Sunday morning worship service in the chapel. It has now become a full-time church with activities throughout each week, described on its website as "a beautiful chapel and community of faith by the sea . . . and a place of refuge from the troubled seas of life," with programs for all ages and mission outreach to the community and internationally.

Tabernacle United Methodist Church

Tabernacle Church, which still meets in its original 1830 building, is well known in the Pungo area, thanks to its annual Lotus Luncheon, its annual Colonial Dinner, and its Christian rock band, "Vantage Point," made up of youth members of the church.

Located next to Tabernacle Creek, home of the exotic American lotus, the church began the Lotus Luncheon in

1955. Because of its city-wide popularity, the luncheon continued even after the lotus flowers died off in the 1980's. Fortunately, the lotus blossoms have recently made a comeback. The Colonial Dinner, begun in 1977, offers traditional Princess Anne County foods and 19th century atmosphere, as well as a bake sale and a bazaar.

❋

ASBURY UNITED METHODIST

CHURCH HISTORY

Rev. John Haynes, the pastor of Asbury United Methodist Church, located on Princess Anne Road (formerly known as Pungo Ridge Road), showed me a copy of the original deed for the church property, recorded in the Clerk's Office of Princess Anne County, Virginia, on September 24, 1872 (Deed Book 50, Page 409). It reads as follows:

"John D. James and Mary Frances, his wife, sold to Thomas Wright, Cornelius Hodges, Noah Cotton, Wilson Barnett, Daniel Murden, and Henry Irwin, Trustees----In trust for the uses and purposes hereinafter named. For the sum of $25, one acre of land, situated in Pungo Township on the Pungo Ridge Road, in Princess Anne County----bounded on the North by the lands of Dennis B. Malbone—on East and South by the lands of John D. James, and on the West by the main road—beginning at a large persimmon tree on the Southwest corner of Malbone's land and running eastward 79 yds [sic] and 2 ft [sic] to a cedar post, thence southward 59 yds and 2 ft to a cedar post, thence westward 9 yds and 2 ft to a cedar post, thence northward along the main road 69 yds and 2 ft to the persimmon tree, place of beginning.

"Unto the sd [sic] Trustees and their successors in office, in fee simple, forever, in trust that the sd premises shall be used, kept, and maintained and disposed of as a place of Divine Worship, for the use of the Ministry and membership of the Methodist Episcopal Church in the United States of America, subject to the Discipline, usage and ministerial appointments of the sd church, as from time to time, authorized and declared by the general Conference of the sd Church and Annual Conference in whose bounds the sd premises are situated."

When I expressed interest in learning about the history of Asbury United Methodist Church, one of the members shared with me the following information, prepared in April 1981.

Asbury United Methodist Church, Pleasant Ridge, Virginia Beach, Virginia, was organized in 1871. It was built in 1872, under the leadership of John D. and Mary Frances James, Thomas Wright, Cornelius Hodges, Noah Cotton, Wilson Barnett, Daniel Murden, and Henry Irvin. The land was purchased for 25 dollars from John D. James and his wife Mary Frances Fentress James. This spot, where the church is still located at present, was in the midst of woods. The members cleared away the land and built the first church of logs, using the timbers that they cleared away. In 1917 the log cabin was torn down and a new frame structure was built under the leadership of Rev. J. J. Dickens.

This church has a long history of use by the Pungo community. During the early 1900's the property was used as an educational center. Later a new school was built by Princess Anne County, which supplied the teachers. The True Reforming Lodge was built on the property, and included some of Asbury's members, among them the Wrights, the Jacksons, the Lovitts, and the Capps. There was also a youth branch of this lodge called the Rose Bud Lodge, which consisted of young boys and girls. The center served as a meeting place for the Good Samaritan Lodge. When the school was destroyed by fire, the lodge served as a school until a new school was built.

The present school was moved from Charity Neck to the church lot with the consent of the county. That building was moved by a mule-drawn wagon with the help of Walter Brock, Frank Brock, Ruben Lamb, and Ernest Jackson. The school was used until 1946. Some of the teachers were Mrs. Parson, Ms. Eva Jones, Ms. Sadie Bright, Mrs. Ruth Forbes, and Mrs. Leliah Holloman, who later became the first principal of Seaboard Elementary, now Princess Anne Elementary School.

In 1944 the church building was blown down by a hurricane. The present building was built from 1947-49 under the leadership of Rev. J. A. Pankey and J. W. Gamble. During the pastorate of Rev. Willie S. Beary, 1954-58, Asbury Church joined the Goldsboro, North Carolina/Newport News, Virginia District of the Central Jurisdiction of The Methodist Church, and the congregation grew to a total of 86 members. It was the only African American Methodist Church in Princess Anne County (now a part of Virginia Beach) at that time, and is currently the only African American United Methodist Church in Virginia Beach.

Asbury Church family joined The United Methodist Church, Virginia Conference, in 1968. The new fellowship hall was added under the leadership of Rev. Godfrey Tate and with the assistance of the District Superintendent, Dr. Carl Sanders.

In November 1971, Asbury Church celebrated its 100th anniversary under the leadership of Rev. Napolean

Graves. Since 1970, the church has added a new fellowship hall, kitchen appliances, the office, folding chairs, the church steeple, repairs and renovations, painted and paneled the sanctuary, and added air conditioning. In May 1979, Asbury celebrated its 107th anniversary and Rev. Franklin D. Caldwell's first year as pastor, with a week of meetings held to give thanks to God for His many blessings.

The old school building has been declared a historical site, and has been partially restored and the exterior painted by the Restoration Committee, chaired by Mr. Ellis Hamberry, with the help of Sheriff Frank Drew, who added desks and chalkboard from the days the school was in use.

Asbury United Methodist Church

The former Pleasant Ridge School

VI.

A FEW MORE PUNGO TALES

MOONSHINE IN PUNGO

(As told by Joe Burroughs)

My cousin Mike Waller suggested that I include a story about moonshine in the next edition of "Pungo Tales." The name that came to my mind was Speed Fentress, who lived on Indian River Road immediately after you go across the West Neck Bridge as you're driving west. Here is what Joe shared:

The Pungo area was known for its many moonshine stills, especially during Prohibition. Joe tells about meeting a fellow from North Carolina at an antique car show. When he saw Joe's old car, he said he once had one like that. Then he asked Joe where he was from, and Joe said, "Pungo."

The man said, "I knew a man in Pungo whose name was Speed Fentress. I used to go to Pungo once a week and visit him. As we sat and talked, I would notice my car would disappear, and after a while it would return. Then Speed would say, 'Okay, it's time for you to go back to North Carolina.' When I got back, I would find 20 gallons of whiskey in my car, and I would sell it back home in North Carolina."

I asked Joe if Speed ever actually had a still in some woods. He said, "Not to my knowledge. He just knew where to buy it and sell it to his customers." He definitely was a businessman. In addition to the country store near the bridge, he ran a camp for migrant workers who came at harvest time to help nearby farmers. He also had a dance hall for African Americans only, although he himself was not African American, and Joe said, "He would not let any white persons go in there."

One additional thing that impressed Joe about him is that when Charity Church building burned down in 1941, Speed Fentress made a major contribution for the rebuilding of the church.

Joe also remembers that Eddie Tatum used to say there are five kinds of whiskey. In other words, there are five things that come out of people who drink whiskey, and they are Cussing, Crying, Fighting, Lying, or Singing, none of which are very productive.

❈

GONE FISHING

(As told by Charlie Griffith)

Some years ago the Wesley Fellowship Sunday School Class of Charity United Methodist Church had a get-together at the beautiful home of Charlie and Ginger Griffith, located on the Back Bay side of Sandbridge Beach, which included a delicious covered-dish supper. Before eating, Charlie took some of us out in the bay on his pontoon boat. It was a beautiful and calm scene out in the water. All of a sudden the nice breeze got a little bit strong and it blew my wife Betty's baseball cap off her head. That was no problem for Charlie because he could easily turn around his boat and go over by the cap and pick it up with his oar, and on our way we went. From a distance we could see several duck blinds scattered throughout parts of the bay.

After cruising around for some 30 minutes or so, we started on our way back to Charlie's dock beside his house. At one point Charlie stopped, turned off the motor, and started telling us about a funny experience he had at that location:

Charlie was fishing at that very place on one occasion with Wayne Davis when they had a lot of luck and caught some wonderful fish. It was beginning to get near dark, so he and Wayne decided to go on in and come back bright and early the next morning and see if they could catch more fish there. They agreed not to tell anyone about their adventure.

Very early the next morning there was a knock at Charlie's door. It was Wayne, ready to go fishing. Quickly they got in the boat and away they went with plenty of bait and a lot of enthusiasm to catch more fish.

Lo and behold, when they got to that same spot there were many boats and fishermen bringing in the fish. Charlie looked at Wayne and asked, "You didn't tell anyone about this place, did you?" Wayne said, "Well, I casually mentioned it to Sonny Gregory." When we heard that, we all started to laugh, especially those of us who grew up around here and remembered Sonny. We recalled Sonny as a jovial and energetic person who was full of life. We could easily picture Sonny telling others about that good fishing hole.

When we got back to the dock we went into the Griffiths' house and had a delicious meal, without any fish!

OCEANA WILL SHINE TONIGHT

The Senior Resource Center sponsored a one-day tour of two historical sites – Pleasant Hall and the Adam Thoroughgood House in Virginia Beach -- on February 13, 2013. What does that have to do with Oceana High School? I will get to that eventually.

Prior to that tour, Dr. Steve Mansfield had made a presentation at the Senior Resource Center about the history of the Village of Kempsville. He explained that James Kemp, a prosperous exporter of tobacco, had owned property at the eastern end of the Elizabeth River. At Kemps Landing there was inspection of tobacco which was being exported in the 1740's. Warehouses were established along the river to store tobacco in hopes that the price would go up. During those days the population of Kempsville was increasing.

Kempsville was the gateway to Princess Anne County from Norfolk until the 20th century. The first four locations of Princess Anne County Courthouse were in the Kempsville area. One of those locations was behind the historic house called "Pleasant Hall," which was built around 1769. It is one of the only four Virginia Beach properties included on both the state and national historic registers. Today, Pleasant Hall belongs to Kempsville Baptist Church, and it is open for visitors to take tours through its beautiful rooms. After the War of Independence, the Kempsville area was in decline and it was decided to move the Courthouse to its present location in 1783, in the geographical center of the county.

After we left Pleasant Hall and the Kempsville area, we visited the Adam Thoroughgood House, built around 1720. It is one of the most famous historical sites of the City of Virginia Beach. It was probably built by one of the descendants of Adam Thoroughgood.

I know you want to know what Oceana High School has to do with all of this. Let me take you back to Pleasant Hall. After we toured that house, we gathered in the large reception room and certain persons spoke to us explaining about the rebuilding of the Village of Kempsville. Among the presentations was one by the builder who is going to remodel the old Kempsville High School building and make it into fine apartments. After showing the plans, he asked if any of the persons present had gone to Kempsville High School, and there were some who told their stories.

Kempsville High School closed in 1954 when it merged with Oceana and Creeds high schools to form Princess Anne High School. The old building served for a number of years as Kemps Landing Middle School, and some persons present indicated that they taught there for some years. Each time someone spoke of having been related to that building, the rest of us applauded.

Finally, I raised my hand and was given the opportunity to speak. I said, "I did not study at Kempsville High School nor did I teach at Kemps Landing Middle School. I went to Oceana High School, and you should all know that Oceana High School was far superior to Kempsville!" There was no applause whatsoever -- just silence. I was even prepared to sing the Oceana High School fight song:

Oceana will shine tonight, Oceana will shine.

Oceana will shine tonight, won't that be fine?

Oceana will shine tonight, Oceana will shine.

When the sun goes down and the moon comes up,

Oceana will shine."

But with all that silence, I just sat down.

JOE BURROUGHS AND

CHOCOLATE FUDGE

When I was growing up in Pungo, Joe's parents, Fred and Malvine Burroughs, had several horses and ponies, which friends and neighbors were often permitted to ride. Many times I was given the opportunity to ride them. It was always fun to ride those horses with Joe.

Now those horses are all gone. Instead of riding horses, Joe and I often ride our bicycles together, and sometimes Stuart Chaplain rides with us. When we ride on the Virginia Beach boardwalk we start at the south end of the beach and park my pickup in the parking lot which allows local residents who are senior citizens to park free of charge. Then we go to the very end of the boardwalk at Rudee Inlet and see the surfers out there in the water waiting patiently for just the right waves to ride into the beach. After we find that everything is all right there, including checking out the nice new restroom, we start to ride toward the north.

The new element related to riding at the boardwalk is that Joe has discovered they have delicious chocolate fudge mixed with peanut butter for sale in a business at the entrance to the fishing pier. As we are riding by that special place, I ask Joe if he wants to stop and get some fudge, but he says, "No, let's do that on the way back. I'll need the energy then more than I do now."

One important element about riding on the boardwalk is the wind. When the wind is behind us and it is actually helping to push us along, it is easy riding and we start to think, "Wow, this sure is nice!" At the north end, we stop for a rest and spend some time "solving the world's problems." When we start back we have to deal with the wind, which was helping us going north, but is now blowing against us. It is much harder to pedal with that wind trying to hold us back, especially now that we are in the year when we turn 80 years old.

As we struggle against the wind, we get a glimpse of the business where they sell that delicious fudge. All of a sudden, Joe starts to ride much faster, leaving me way behind. The last time we rode there, when I finally got to Joe's favorite fudge stop, I said to him, "Joe, do you remember when we used to ride horseback, and as we got near the stables, the horses started running out of control as fast as they could?" He responded, "Yes, and if we didn't bend over as they went through the stable door, we'd get knocked off." I concluded, "When you speeded up as you saw the fudge store, you reminded me of those horses running out of control toward the stable!"

GROWING OLD IN PUNGO

Chapter Two is about "Growing Up in Pungo," and this book ends with the question, "What's it like growing old in Pungo?"

When my wife was on the Board of Trustees of Ferrum College near Franklin, Virginia, I went with her to meetings as her chauffeur. While she was in the meetings, I walked around the campus and talked with people and did some reading in the library.

One day as I was sitting in the lounge of the library building, a student walked up to me and asked, "What's it like being old?" Instead of reacting in anger, I decided to do some quick thinking and praying, and came up with the response, "Well, if you've lived a good life and have good memories, it's all right being old. But if you've lived a bad life and have bad memories, it's not so good being old!" He said, "Hmm, that makes sense." I asked him to sit down and talk for a few minutes. He told me something about his life, and I shared that I'm a retired pastor. He mentioned that he only goes to church at Christmas and on Easter Sunday.

A few months later I served as chaplain on a cruise ship. In one of my sermons, I told that story. A lady raised her hand and I stopped for her to say something. She said, "My husband here beside me is 97 years old." I left the pulpit and went over to where he was seated (he looked like he was 67) and asked him, "What's it like being old?" He quickly answered, "Well, if you've lived a good life and have good memories, it's all right being old." My rapid response was, "I've heard that somewhere before."

If you've been fortunate enough to grow up in Pungo or some similar place, and have lived a good life, it's all right growing old. Even though we no longer know everybody in

Pungo as we did years ago, there still exists the spirit of helping each other in times of need. People of our churches are constantly praying for our neighbors in need and looking for ways to help out. Our Senior Resource Center provides a place for senior citizens to gather and encourage one another, in addition to providing many helpful programs and materials about resources available in the City of Virginia Beach.

Pungo is a great place to grow old!

-- Walt Whitehurst, Pungo, May 2013

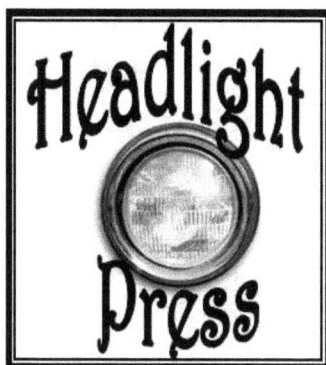

HEADLIGHT PRESS
6500 CLITO ROAD
STATESBORO, GEORGIA 30461
912-587-4400

www.ingramcontent.com/pod-product-compliance
Lightning Source LLC
Chambersburg PA
CBHW052103270326

41931CB00012B/2864